NICK WALPERT

G.E.T.
CUSTOMER SERVICE
EXCELLENCE

CREATE WORLD-CLASS CUSTOMER SERVICE STANDARDS

CONTENTS

Welcome to Juicy Burgers Restaurant Customer Service Guide

Juicy Burgers Restaurants (JBR) is a large, successful and highly visible food service company with a proud past and a promising future.

We serve many different people from all segments of society and our future growth hinges on our ability to give every customer the BEST service possible. We value our diverse customer base and are committed to treating all customers and fellow employees with dignity and respect.

We're glad you have decided to join our team. Our team consists of people who enjoy providing customers with an unbeatable dining experience.

Today people have many choices.

What makes people choose Juicy Burgers over its competitors? A value priced menu with many choices might bring people in once, but excellent customer service will keep them coming back. People naturally go to places where they are treated well. A reputation for excellent customer service takes efforts on all fronts, from the frontline providing a friendly smile to the cook preparing a quality product. At Juicy Burgers fostering outstanding customer service is every employee's responsibility. Regardless of job title, everyone plays an integral role in the customers overall experience. Therefore, it is important that each employee does his or her own part to guarantee the customer receives the exceptional customer service that Juicy Burgers promises to deliver. Your effort is key to Juicy Burgers success. Social media plays a role as well. Our customers love to post!

You will be expected to be very knowledgeable about all products we sell, so you can assist your customers in making educated decision.

How the Training Works

First your manager will give you a complete orientation to working here at Creative Host Services. You will be introduced to your brand concept and review our employee handbook. Your manager will help guide you through your training and evaluate your performance.

Steps of Training

The training follows a five step learning process (RDDPR).

- Read
- Discuss
- Demonstrate
- Practice
- Review

Read available materials; Brand Standards, Handbooks, Posted Memo's and Job Aids. It is helpful to learn basic information before you begin training. This gives you an idea of what to expect and introduces basic terminology. It may prompt questions if you see something different then from what was read.

Discuss any questions you have with your Trainer or Manager.

Demonstrate. Your Trainer will perform the task and describe each step. Your Trainer will tell you why you do things a certain way.

Practice your skills. Your Trainer will ask you to describe the steps of the task. He/she will observe your performance.

Review with your trainer areas of improvement and success.

Your first few days at work will be devoted to learning and providing Customer Service Excellence in your job.

Customer Service is one of the most powerful marketing tools available. It helps build business and is essential in maintaining the Creative Host Services commitment to superior quality and excellence. Outstanding service is vital to our success. Why? Because you're not just selling a product....you're selling an experience. The Wow Experience!

Juicy Burgers has a reputation as the unparalleled leader in the Hamburger and quick serve restaurant market. This reputation shapes each customer's expectations in the area of service. Every customer who walks into our business expects a service level equal to the quality of the product. In addition, each customer as a personal agenda: his/her individual expectations of exceptional customer service. For some it may be friendliness, product knowledge, or cleanliness. For others it may be speed of service or an ability to efficiently resolve complaints. Exceptional service is based upon satisfying a challenging combination of brand expectation and personal preference/lifestyle needs. When you consistently deliver a level of service that exceeds your customer's expectations, you build brand loyalty that surpasses the competition.

Our Service Goal: **To provide exceptional service to every customer every time.**

To achieve this goal, we have developed a Customer Service Program. This section will detail the program by first discussing our customer, then describing the three elements that comprise exceptional service: Service Standards; Execution and Environment. Finally, this section will explain how these elements need to be supported through training, measurement, and service recovery.

The Customer

Providing exceptional customer service requires a basic understanding of customers. By understanding people's habits, patterns, interests, and concerns, you can better position your service, promotions and customer care to meet their needs and encourage their patronage.

Research indicates that the core and most loyal customers are families and traveling professionals from any age group with interests in sports, theater, music, books and entertainment. This audience recognizes the superior quality of our products and expects the same level of service. Of course, the demographic makeup of customers in your local market may vary significantly.

Demographics aside, it is important to recognize, and respect people as individuals with differing needs and expectations. This kind of treatment is gratifying to customers, making them feel good about themselves and our products and service.

To fully appreciate the impact of customer service on your business and you and your team's performance, consider the following research findings. In the retail industry as a whole:

- One out of every four customers is unhappy with the service they receive
- Only five percent of dissatisfied customers complain

- The dissatisfied customer will tell 12 additional people about his/her experience

- The satisfied customer will tell five additional people about his/her experience

- Dissatisfied customers who do not complain will usually not return to your store or restaurant

- Exceptional service can insure 50-80% of your repeat business

- It costs eight times less to service a repeat customer than it does to establish the same level of satisfaction with a new customer

- Pleasing a dissatisfied customer will result in a more loyal customer

Obviously, it is in your restaurant's best interest to serve customers well to keep them coming back. In light of the damage that even one dissatisfied customer can cause, the customer still needs an opportunity to express his or her dissatisfacwtion and have their concerns addressed. Whatever it takes to please a dissatisfied customer usually proves to be cost effective in the long run.

We need to recognize each customer as a partner. Without the customer there is no business; without the customer, the best environment, the finest products, the highest service standards and execution of those standards mean nothing. Whether customers help build your business, or become obstacles to growth, it is largely determined by your customer service practices. For all of these reasons, it makes sense to remember you are empowered to deliver the highest standard of service possible to each and every customer.

The Elements of Exceptional Service

In offering our products, certain standards must be maintained and projected though attitude, action, and the overall environment. Anything less falls short of the Creative Juicy Burgers experience in Exceptional Customer Service.

Service Standards

To provide the Juicy Burgers experience, we have developed a philosophy consisting of four service standards. These standards are guidelines to assist in customer service decision-making. Integrated into your daily business practices, they send a powerful, positive message to our customer.

These service standards also give employees a sense of the Juicy Burgers image and their role in creating and maintaining it. Introduced to employees on their first day and constantly reinforced thereafter, these standards are the tools that can build excellent customer relations.

The four service standards:

1. **Value the Customer.** Customers are your most valuable commodity, and they'll like you and your restaurant all the more for letting them know it. That's why every employee action should focus on making the customer feel special.

This should be expressed not only by what you say, but also how you behave; non-verbal communications are often the most telling. Ways to make the customer feel valued include: giving customers undivided attention; being courteous; smiling; not holding side conversations or phone conversations while customers are waiting: and thanking them for coming in. Treat customers as you would like to be treated.

2. **Be Friendly.** Friendly, courteous, attentive, and smiling employees with positive attitudes enhance the whole experience. They also raise the customer's comfort level, and increase his/her receptiveness to product suggestions.

3. **Be Knowledgeable.** Customers want to be informed. By demonstrating knowledge of products, recipes, and promotions, and adding personal enthusiasm, you will educate the customer and expand his/her own appreciation of our products.

4. **Provide Efficient Service.** Customer needs should be satisfied quickly and efficiently without jeopardizing customer goodwill. Employees should make every effort to be prompt with those in a hurry, and take time, when possible, with those who are undecided or not in a rush. A sense of urgency in your work routine will let the customer know you care about their experience.

Commit yourself and your teammates to valuing the customer, and providing friendly, knowledgeable, and efficient service, and you'll be well on your way to creating a successful and rewarding customer experience.

Role and Responsibilities

- Work safely!

- Treat all customers with a "Can-Do" attitude

- Take and serve orders with a smile

- Suggestive sell

- Have a neat and clean appearance with the proper uniform

- Stock and clean work areas "as-you-go"

- Follow standards and procedures at all times

- Treat all customers consistently in a friendly, interested, and helpful manner

Service Standards Execution

Once you're familiar with the service standards, you need to learn how to execute them in actual customer situations.

A typical customer transaction is broken down into four stages, each of which utilizes one or more of the Juicy Burgers Service Standards.

The four stages of a customer transaction are:

G = **Greet the Customer**
E = **Execute the Sale**
T = **Thank the Customer**

1. **Greet the Customer.** The customer, as a guest in your restaurant, is to be greeted warmly the moment he/she

enters. Below are some guidelines for welcoming the customer:

- Smile

- Acknowledge the customer as soon as possible

- Greet the customer in a warm, friendly manner, than ask an opening question to start the sale

- Give the customer undivided attention and maintain eye contact

    - "Hi! How may I help you?"

    - "Welcome to ….. My name is ….. Would you like to try ….."

    - (During busy times) A warm smile and …. "Thanks for your patience. We'll be with you as soon as possible."

2. **Execute the Sale.** Building the sale is the process of determining what will be prepared or given to the customer. This is done by asking questions, responding to inquiries, and offering suggestions.

First, establish the customer's needs.

Examples:

- "How may I help you"?

- "Would you like to try our special today"?

Some customers will know exactly what they want; others will need help in deciding. In either case, offer sample tastes if available as one way to educate the customer.

Once the customer's initial order is confirmed, then you can then attempt to build upon the sale. Here, employees sell by making suggestions such as the following:

- "Would you like a Large"?
- Offer a dessert if the customer orders a entrée
- Know your specials

Listen carefully and confirm the order with the customer to avoid misunderstanding. By demonstrating interest in the customer throughout the sale, a rapport and level of trust are created.

3. **Prepare the Order.** Once the basic order is established, the employee should focus on providing efficient service while creating an appealing product. If the product is Grab-N-Go or already prepared then just ring up the order.

4. **Thank the Customer and Close the Sale.** When closing the sale, ask the customer, "Would you like anything else?". Refrain from, "Is that it?", which to many customers sounds discourteous. When the sale is complete, you may want to repeat the order back to the customer as you key in to the POS or register. For example: "That was a half-pound burger and two large chocolate shakes." This lets the customer know that he/she is being charged for what was ordered.

Then follow the steps below:

- Announce the total sale

- Announce the denomination of the bill received (i.e. "out of $20") and place on the register ledge.

- Count the change back to the customer aloud

- Put the money in the register and close the cash drawer

- Complete the transaction and reinforce good feelings by thanking the customers and asking to see them again soon.

The Environment of your Restaurant says a lot about Customer Service

The condition of your restaurant speaks greatly about you and your teammates with regards to cleanliness, quality, and safety. Upon entering, a customer immediately forms a perception of a service experience based on the environment in which it will take place. That initial perception will either reinforce or diminish the customer's expectations, which may significantly affect his/her buying decisions. In essence, the environment sets the stage for the rest of the transaction. That's why an attractive, clean, and safe environment is just as important as a pleasant and positive customer interaction.

Your environment should invite customers inside. Everything from décor to the temperature should be appealing. After all, people are coming to your restaurant for enjoyment.

Safety plays a major role in creating this appealing environment. Your customers place their trust in your team's ability to deliver a product and environment that will not harm them. All products and food handling standards must be followed at all times.

For our purposes, environment is defined as every element inside and outside that is within the control or view of our employees. Maintaining environment quality is the responsibility of every employee. In evaluating your environment, consider the following:

- Cleanliness
- Uniforms
- Displays
- Counters
- Equipment
- Floors
- Tables/Chairs
- Temperature
- Sound & Lighting
- Signage
- Product Appearance

Supporting Customer Service Standards

The final portion of the Customer Service Program is to support the establishment and execution of the service standards and the maintenance of a safe, clean, and attractive environment by implementing the following:

- Training

- Measuring Service Quality
- Service Recovery System

Training

Providing our customers with the best possible eating experience takes concentrated effort. Human Resources will coordinate and provide various training in all areas, especially in the area of Customer Service. We will help our employees find the passion for delivering exceptional customer service. In order for that, they must first develop an understanding of what it is, its value, and how to provide it. Such awareness and skills are provided through customer service training.

Our Executive Directors, Regional Directors and General Managers play a vital role here by demonstrating a commitment to customer service standards and training, and setting a positive example through their actions. They will be working hard to help you provide excellent customer service.

Measuring Service Quality

Measuring the quality of service allows us to evaluate your unit's effectiveness and performance from the most valuable point of view: your customer's. To facilitate the measuring of service quality we have several manners. First, we conduct our own QA inspections and Audits. Second, we will use various external programs such as Mystery Shops, Customer Comment Cards, Toll-Free Numbers and other direct customer feedback systems. Your unit will receive feedback on these comments from corporate.

Service Recovery

There are times when an employee fails to meet customers' expectations. The customer may voice disappointment or express dissatisfaction. Because we honor the "customer is always right" policy, it is imperative that the customer's concern be acknowledged and handled to the customer's satisfaction….and, the sooner the better. To do this efficiently and effectively, a set of Service Recovery procedures has been established for your unit. Every employee is responsible for good service to our customers.

Whenever there is a problem or customer complaint you should notify your manager to ensure the issue is addressed and resolved. Here are some general employee guidelines upon which we base our own Service Recovery system:

- A verbal complaint is an opportunity for the employee to rectify a situation and please the customer

- Listen carefully without interruption. Resolving a complaint positively influences that customer's repeat business and other customers in the restaurant at that time

- Be helpful and courteous when answering a question or complaint. Try to find out what the customer is expecting and what will make him/her happy. Never send the customer away unhappy.

- If an employee is unable to resolve a complaint or satisfy the customer, he/she should get the manager.

Uniform and Grooming Standards

When our customers enter our restaurants, they expect not only a quality product, but also a pleasant dining experience. Employees are required to meet the uniform and grooming standards at all times to ensure consistency in the application of Juicy Burgers appearance requirements. Please contact your manager or Human Resources Department for any religious or disability accommodation requests.

Proper dress attire consists of a clean, pressed uniform to include:

- Black pants or skirt (no more than 2" above or below knee)
- Company uniform top
- Dark socks or flesh tone/black pantyhose
- Black non-slip soled, leather upper shoes with no open toes or heels

Personal Hygiene

Good personal hygiene is essential. Hands must be clean with no false fingernails. Nails are to be trimmed to a reasonable length with clear or natural color polish when appropriate. Make up must be light in texture and natural looking. Hair should be clean, trimmed and restrained. Men should be clean-shaven with mustaches and sideburns neatly trimmed. Beards are not permitted except in medically documented cases or due to religious reasons.

Jewelry

Appropriate jewelry includes: two hand rings, wristwatch and one pair of earrings that does not dangle below the ear. No facial jewelry for nose, tongue, lip, etc. are allowed during the work shift and should be removed while working your shift. Necklaces are to be worn inside shirts/blouses.

We certainly respect everyone's definition of what is acceptable, but it is management's responsibility to ensure a uniform professional appearance. Management reserves the right to determine what is an appropriate dress code.

Service Priorities

When our restaurants are busy, you will have to decide which tasks are completed first. To help you, we have listed some service priorities in order of importance.

Top Priorities

- Great and acknowledge customers
- Take Order
- Accept payment
- Smile

Secondary Priorities

- Serve hot food hot, cold food cold
- Service with a smile
- Answer the phone

While top priorities are correct, that assumes that all four situations come up simultaneously. In general terms, customers should be served right away and on a first come first served basis.

Speed of Service

Whether customers have a long wait for their plane or in a hurry to get the gate they have a limited amount of time and no one likes to wait. It is our job to serve customers as courteously and efficiently as possible. Everyone will recognize the efforts you put forth to service them as fast as possible without giving the feeling of being rushed.

Learn your Menu

Learning your menu is a very important step in becoming successful in providing excellent customer service. You can use the menu as a sales tool to suggest different menu items and increase your sales.

Customer Relations

This is it! Customer relations is the reason we need you. Here at Creative Host Services, we are committed to treating all customers and fellow employees with dignity and respect. We do not discriminate against any customer or employee on the basis of race, color, religion, national origin, disability, sex, sexual orientation, or age.

Let's look at some ways you can enhance your people skills, therefore helping ensure Creative Host Services success as well as your own.

Behavior Models

A "behavior model" is a learning tool which provides action steps that you can use to do something differently. It's like a road map that gets you from one place to the next. It helps you answer: "How can I interact more effectively with my customers?" and "What can I do differently?"

The following two models are learning tools that will help improve your interactions with our customers. The tools are user-friendly and flexible. They are easy to remember and can be applied in a variety of situations.

Prevention Model

The Prevention Model is designed to help you prevent guest complaints. The focus of the Prevention Model is consistent service to all customers. Treating all customers consistently results in better customer service experience, which also results in fewer complaints of poor service or discrimination, whether actual or perceived. The Prevention Model is a positive, proactive approach you can use.

C= Be	**<u>C</u>onsistent and Communicate**
A = Be	**<u>A</u>ttentive**
N = Meet the	**<u>N</u>eeds (of customers)**
C =	**Be Consistent and Communicate**

* Treat every customer with dignity and respect

* Apply Creative Host Services policies to every customer

* Attend to every customer – be polite, sincere, and courteous

* Meet the needs of every customer

A = **Be Attentive**

* Talk with customers; listen for facts and signs of how the person is feeling

* Observe the customers' body language and emotions

* Make eye contact, smile, and say thank you

N = **Meet the Needs**

* Listen for understanding

* Ask questions – seek their ideas or suggestions

* Respond – take action and use customer
  ideas when possible

* Explain the situation

To assist you in remembering the Prevention Model, use the acronym **C.A.N.. "We CAN" achieve exceptional customer service at Creative Host Services by preventing customer dissatisfaction.**

Intervention Model

The Intervention Model is used when "something has gone wrong" in an interaction with a customer. You have the responsibility and authority to solve customer complaints. You need to respond and take whatever action is needed to solve the problem and make the customer happy. It builds on the three A's: Acknowledge, Apologize and Act. Like the Prevention Model it answers the question, "What can I do differently? What actions can I take?

Acknowledge

- Meet the guest at eye level

- Listen to the guest describe the problem without interrupting

- Ask questions if you are unsure in a sensitive and inoffensive manner. (You do not want the customer to feel as if you are trying to prove them wrong.)

- Double-check for understanding

- Describe back to the guest what you understand as the problem

Apologize

- Tell the customer you are sorry the problem occurred

- Explain what happened

- Apologize again and assure them it will be corrected

- Thank the customer for calling the problem to your attention

- Don't make excuses, or blame other staff associates

Act

- Ask the customer how you can "make it right", or improve the situation

- Tell the customer what you can do to solve the problem

- DO IT!!

- Report your actions to the customer

Action Alternatives

There may be times the customer's complaint appears invalid. It doesn't matter whether the complaint seems valid to us or not. All that matters is that the guest is not happy and we do not want our customers leaving our units dissatisfied. Some things you may do to satisfy your customers are:

- Substitute or exchange an item

- Deduct the amount of the item from the check if replacement is not an option for the customer

- Give additional items to satisfy the customers expectation

- Use common sense

- Follow your Manager's guidelines

- It is the management teams responsibility, as well as all employees in the restaurant to ensure that our customers leave totally satisfied

- The Manager will ensure all policies and procedures are applied consistently to all customers, without regard to race, religion, color, gender, age, or national origin.

- If a customer is upset, do not rush to offer free food or service, but try to solve the problem by listening to the customer, apologizing for their experience, and acting to address the guest's needs and concerns. Remember, offering free food isn't the way to satisfy angry customers. Sometimes customers just want to know that you will listen and that you care.

Greeting/Acknowledgment

Excellent customer service begins with the first person the customer meets. If you're that person, you are responsible for greeting the customer in a way that makes them feel welcome and appreciated.

It is very important to set a positive first impression of the restaurant and yourself for each guest coming to our business. Let customers know you are truly glad to see them. Every employee needs to show a sense of urgency when greeting customers. Creative Host Services timing standard for greeting customers is immediately upon them walking up to our units. Greeting and acknowledging our customers promptly creates two perceptions, that they are welcome and we are ready to serve them.

The following are some other customer service tips:

- Smile
- Welcome them with "Good morning/afternoon/evening" or "Hi, Welcome to 'state your brand name'. Use your own greeting that makes every customer feel welcome and appreciated. Make an effort not to sound mechanical.
- Make it a point to make eye contact when speaking

Answering the Telephone

When answering the phone, the same warm, friendly greeting is standard. Identify the location they have called. In a polite and friendly tone, you might say:

"Good morning. Creative Croissant at LAX. This is (name), how may I help you?

It is also important to maintain security when answering the phone. Use these rules when answering callers questions.

- Never tell the caller or say there is not a manager on duty. You might say, "I'm sorry the Manager is not available to take your call right now, may I take a message".
- If the caller wants to speak to a manager who is not on duty, take a message and have the Manager return the call.

- Never give full names, home addresses, phone numbers, or work schedules of employees or managers to callers. If a caller insists refer the call to your manager.

- Never give references on current or former employees. Refer these calls to the Manager or Human Resources

Handling Employee Calls

- Explain to the caller that you will give a message to the employee who may return the call on his/her next break

- Take down the message and give it to the employee

- Emergency calls should always be put through to the person concerned

Shift Responsibility

There are certain things that must be done before, during, and after the shift to ensure that your customers' needs are met.

Personal Appearance

Are you presenting a favorable self-image?

- Uniform is correct, clean and wrinkle free
- You are wearing your name tag
- Your shoes have rubber non-slip soles
- Hair is neatly groomed and won't require handling during work
- Hands and fingernails are clean

Attitude

Prepare yourself mentally to be friendly and helpful to your customers. Some days this may take extra effort on your part.

Unit Presentation

At the start of your shift, check all areas to ensure they are properly cleaned and supplied so you are prepared to give your customers the best possible experience. Each employee has the responsibility to our customers to make sure everything is cleaned and stocked. See your manager for specific job duties.

Clean-As-You-Go

Keep your work area clean and stocked throughout your shift. By doing so, you are ensuring the items your guests need will be on hand. Plus, the restaurant looks good for our customers.

Sidework

Sidework refers to the routine cleaning and stocking that prepares us to serve our customers. Each associate has certain sidework duties that they need to complete each shift. Sidework duties are determined by the shift you work as directed by the Manager. Being prepared for your customers also shows them that you care about their dining experience. Sidework must be completed while you are being paid (on the clock).

Taking care of customers is your first priority. We never expect you to neglect your customers to complete sidework. Teamwork between shifts is important to maintain smooth and efficient service to our customers. You are expected to complete your sidework duties before the end of your shift.

Emergencies

In emergency situations, by acting immediately, calmly, and following these procedures, you will be able to ensure the safety of customers and team associates. In this topic you will learn some important information to help you in case an emergency should arise.

Emergency Phone Numbers

- Police
- Fire
- Ambulance
- Managers' home phone numbers
- Regional Director of Operations
- Human Resources

These numbers should be posted in the back room.

Handling Injuries

Minor first aid to employees should only be administered by a qualified person. In case of customer injury get the Manager immediately. If the Manager is not present follow these guidelines:

1. Remain calm. Be courteous and show concern.

2. Ask the customer "Are you all right?" and "What would you like me to do?" Don't call the paramedics unless

requested by the customer or a member of his/her party. The exception to this is when a customer is alone and unable to respond.

3. Don't move the injured customer. This may make the injuries more severe. The exception to this is when they are in a hazardous location. If they are bleeding from the nose or mouth, roll them over on their side to prevent choking or suffocation.

4. After you have taken care of the injured customer you will need to get the following information.

- Name
- Address
- Phone Number

Fire Procedures

If a fire breaks out in the unit, you are responsible for the safety of yourself, customers and other employees.

To do this you must know:

- The location of all emergency exits and shut offs (water, gas, electrical).
- The location of fire extinguishers.
- How to operate fire extinguishers, including the fire control system in the kitchen.

Ask your manager to explain these to you. If a small fire breaks out in the unit, use a fire extinguisher and aim at the base of the fire. If you are unable to put out the fire:

1. Immediately call the Fire Department

2. Evacuate the restaurant

3. Close any doors to stop the fire from spreading

4. Call your manager or Regional Director of Operations

Suggestive Selling

Suggestive Selling requires you to be knowledgeable and provide ordering assistance to your guests. Many of your customers may not even be aware of their food wants. Being able to fill these wants is truly providing excellent service. By making additional food suggestions, you are communicating to your customers, "I want to fill all your dining needs, I'm interested in you".

We sometimes do a good job in suggestive selling, but there is always room for improvement. Some of our customers not being suggestively sold any additional items. The areas needing improvement are: suggesting entrees, offering desserts, suggesting additional beverages, and suggesting a new item or special. Doing these things consistently, with all our customers, will enhance the customer's dining experience and result in a higher check average.

Points to Suggestive Selling

1. Know your menu or offerings:

- You must know what's on our menu so you can suggest appropriate items

- If the item is prepared you must know how it is prepared

- Try different food items, have personal favorites to recommend

2. Use descriptive words that create a mental picture: words like delicious, tasty, tender, etc.

3. Use our props, the pictures on our menu and table tents help make selling easy

4. Use the right words at the right time

- Time your suggestions appropriately; don't offer an appetizer after your customer has already ordered their entrée, offer it with a beverage

- Anticipate your customers' needs such as a hot bowl of soup on a cold day

- Phrase your questions carefully; offer choices and ask "either or" questions.

- Use script cards for the appropriate day part

- Compliment your customers choice and make them feel good about their choice

Alcohol: Selling It Safely

We have a legal obligation to comply with all aspects of the liquor code in the states and localities where we do business. The liquor code is a set of laws that govern the sales of alcoholic beverages. Businesses must have a license to serve alcohol. The license gives us the right and privilege to sell alcoholic beverages. It is a criminal act to violate the laws in the liquor code.

By law, servers have the right and responsibility to refuse service to any person who:

- Appears to be intoxicated
- Is under legal drinking age
- Is a known, habitual intoxicated person

Failure to comply with liquor code laws is considered a criminal act and may be subject to fine, imprisonment and termination of employment with Creative Host Services in addition to the liquor license being revoked.

Civil Liability

Besides complying with the liquor code and federal law, there is civil liability involved with the service of alcohol. Civil liability (or third party liability) refers to the responsibility an owner, manager and employee has in the case of injury or damage caused by a person whom they helped intoxicate. Although the owners or operators themselves have not directly caused the injury, as the "third party", they may be held liable for contributing to the circumstances that allowed the injury to occur. Civil lawsuits are more difficult to defend because the criterion establishing quilt is not as strict. These settlements in these types of lawsuits are typically high because of litigation costs, perceived "deep pockets" of an establishment and because of punitive damages sought for injury or loss.

Third party lawsuits are brought to court under the legal concept of negligence. Negligence is the failure to exercise reasonable care used by a prudent person under similar circumstances. "Reasonable care" is a vague term, and of great importance to the hospitality industry. An establishment must be able to demonstrate in all ways possible that it has exercised reasonable care in it policies and operations. To help assure that reasonable care is exercised, Creative Host Services has adopted certain practices which are outlined:

1. No employee will serve an alcoholic beverage to any person under 21 years of age or to a visibly intoxicated person.

2. Every customer appearing under the age of 30 and ordering an alcoholic beverage is required to present valid identification proving they are 21 or older.

3. All employees will notify a manager when a customer shows visible signs of intoxication. The server or manger will discontinue service in a friendly manner and offer alternative refreshment.

4. All employees will record these incidents as refusal of service on a Memo for Record.

5. No employee will serve more than one drink to a customer at a time.

6. All employees who serve alcoholic beverages will receive training and education in alcohol awareness and policy.

7. Any violation of the Liquor Code is grounds for immediate dismissal.

Summary

Customers will come back to us because we take customer service seriously. We have high standards and know our success depends on how well you provide for your customers. You can increase customer visitations and your sales and profits if your customers' experiences are fun and enjoyable.

Many times you may be the only employee that a customer may see during their visit, thus, it is important that you make a good first and last impression. Your fast, courteous service and attitude is some of the main reasons our customers keep coming back to us.

Thank you for your hard work and support as together we will all be successful.

If you have any questions regarding Customer Service Standards, be sure to ask your manager or contact your Human Resources Department.

NICK R. WALPERT

BIOGRAPHY – FOUNDER/CEO, JUICY BURGERS RESTAURANTS

NICK WALPERT is a persuasive professional speaker and World Business Leader, with an extensive background in both small and big business. A forty year veteran of the corporate world, Nick Walpert reinvented corporate execution, continually setting the standards of excellence while expanding his interests in business – former executive with companies such as EU Multi-National Multirama, Sambo's Restaurants, Denny's Restaurants, McDonalds, Pyramid Beer & Alehouses, Sudwerks Beer, Winchell's Donuts, Jack-in-the-Box,

Kentucky Fried Chicken, Mrs. Fields Cookies, Haagen Dazs Ice Cream, Ghirardelli Chocolate, Good Guys Electronics, CompUSA, Kaiser Healthcare, Daddy Dough Donuts, Juicy Burgers Restaurants, Aloha Ice Cream, Dunkin Donuts, Host Travel Services, DaVita Healthcare, Godfathers Pizza, Wendy's International, bebe Fashion and Kaiser Foundation Hospitals.

As the founder and CEO of Juicy Burgers Restaurants, Nick Walpert is called by Fortune 100 companies to speak, engage motivate; start up corporate and big business corporations for consultations and support for change management, organizational change, executive coaching and providing unique insights into managing a world-class brand. He is the author of the book; **G.E.T. Customer Service Excellence** which he teaches to Corporate America. He motivates employees and managers alike to understand how to provide world class Customer Service consistently in any retail business. Like a master craftsman, Nick is adept at identifying broken links and executing solutions yielding big returns on both top and bottom lines. For the last 40 years and with laser precision, Nick Walpert has rebuilt corporations from the inside out defining the **"Customer Experience"** and how to achieve world-class execution. His rare ability to spot emerging retail, repair broken and poorly managed companies and merchandising trends and insight into the desires of the American consumer has generated growth for retail leaders expanding the definition of retailing in many Fortune 500 companies, including hospitality, retail and services industries delivering customer service excellence.

Nick Walpert attributes much of his success to the training he received in his first-managerial-job as Manager at McDonalds. The McDonald's training programs and management creation systems is one of the foundational elements of his success today. Walpert's humanitarian efforts, his entrepreneurial acumen and his retail vision have been widely recognized in the business community worldwide. He is also the founder of Advanced Renovation Services, MedSpa Boutique and Surgery America. Nick opened his first retail restaurant business at the age of 18 back in 1978; Juicy Burgers Restaurants was born. Nick Walpert is one of corporate America's true living legends and one of the world's most highly rated speakers. He is available for booking either half day at $25,000 or full day at $50,000 anywhere worldwide.

Nick has been solving common and uncommon business problems as well as inspiring individual students and business people to approach today's challenges with purpose and action. His dynamic style and real-life examples allow participants to visualize real solutions. Using some of the same secrets as Sam Walton, the Founder and Chairman of Wal-Mart and Debbie Fields, the Founder of Mrs. Fields Cookies changing the way America does business through excellence in execution.

His international experience with corporate executives around the world has given Nick a unique perspective on business in today's global economy. He brings his own wisdom and experience to the podium and shares what he has mined from the combined knowledge of hundreds of America's greatest corporate minds to create a singular, memorable learning experience that is unequalled in power and scope. Every business that is serious about meeting the challenges of the 21ˢᵗ Century needs to hear what Nick Walpert has to say teaching employees from all fields in customers service excellence through his book, G.E.T. Customer Service Handbook.

Walpert's presentations are both inspirational and motivational. He believes that his new adventure as a professional speaker provides the perfect opportunity to share his executive experiences, his passion for brand excellence and very importantly, it affords him the chance to truly make a difference to today's corporations from the executive team to the front-line employees. If your company wants the improve customer service experience and build sales you need Nick and his book teaching the secrets to happy customers and raising top line revenues.

From major food and beverage companies to industrial manufacturers to healthcare organizations to popular retailers to global telecommunications powers, a diverse group of clients have sought out and received Walpert's business management and marketing expertise. Walpert provides through speaking engagements his clients with the guidance they need to move their marketing efforts from hoping to planning, from art to science, from guessing to knowing, and from random success to planned success.

More recently, Mr. Walpert served as General Manager and President of Multirama, the largest computer and retail consumer electronics giant in Greece; (the Best Buy of Greece) Nick grew this world-class brand through proven leadership and his revolutionary set of principles that are transforming this computer manufacturer and retail stores business model into an even larger powerhouse in the electronics world. Working with the world's largest manufacturer's such as: Sony, HP, Philips, Belkin, Creative, Logitech, Altec, Apple, Olympus, Nikon, Pentax, Kodak, Panasonic, Canon, Fuji, Toshiba, Samsung, JVC, Vector, LG, Acer, Dell, Fujitsu Siemens, Asus, Seagate, Google World, Microsoft and Gigabyte, just to name a few.

Nick Walpert is in great demand for public speaking, often addressing business organizations, especially the world's largest from the Global 1000 to Fortune 100 with his inspirational messages. Despite all of these high-profile activities, you will find Nick Walpert very down to earth, friendly, compassionate and continually curious about the world around him – he is a true modern adventurer.

As a professional speaker and leadership trainer, Nick frequently addresses large and small businesses as well as college and high school students. In addition to being a prolific motivational speaker, Nick has also released several audio CD series and authored the book,

"G.E.T. Customer Service Excellence."

He brings his dynamic energy and real-life experience to his compelling seminars, reaching each participant with a message of attitude, achievement and action.

To book Nick Walpert for your next corporate or seminar event

call 702-981-7310 or
Email to: nick@juicyburgers.net
JuicyBurgers.net